CONTENTS

Where do ghosts swim?
In the Dead Sea.

What did the vampire doctor say?
Necks please!

Did you hear about the banshee who wanted to be an actress?
She did a scream test.

What does a dragon call a knight wearing armour?
Tinned food!

LAUGH OUT LOUD!

THE MONSTER FUN JOKE BOOK

Sean Connolly and Kay Barnham

FRANKLIN WATTS

LONDON · SYDNEY

First published in 2012 by Franklin Watts

Copyright © 2012 Arcturus Publishing Limited

Franklin Watts
338 Euston Road
London
NW1 3BH

Franklin Watts Australia
Level 17/207 Kent Street, Sydney, NSW 2000

Produced by Arcturus Publishing Limited,
26/27 Bickels Yard, 151–153 Bermondsey Street, London SE1 3HA

Editor: Joe Harris
Illustrations: Adam Clay and Dynamo Design
Layout Design: Notion Design

A CIP catalogue record for this book is available from the British Library.

Dewey Decimal Classification Number: 818.6'02-dc23

ISBN: 978 1 4451 1492 7

Franklin Watts is a division of Hachette Children's Books, an Hachette UK company.
www.hachette.co.uk

Printed in China

SL001831EN
Supplier 03, Date 0512, Print Run 1963

MONSTER FUN

What do you get if you cross a vampire and a circus entertainer ?
Someone who goes straight for the juggler!

What do you get if you cross a vampire with a mummy?
Something you wouldn't want to unwrap!

What do ghosts eat for dinner?
Goulash!

How do ghosts begin business letters?
'Tomb it may concern…'

Why didn't the skeleton fight the monster?
He didn't have the guts!

What has a pointy hat, a broomstick and a blue face?
A witch holding her breath.

MONSTER FUN

How can you tell when there's a giant monster under your bed?
When your nose touches the ceiling.

What happened to the vampire with bad breath?
His dentist told him to gargoyle twice a day!

What do vampires do at eleven o'clock every night?
They have a coffin break.

What was written on the robot's tombstone?
Rust in pieces!

How does Frankenstein's monster sit in a chair?
Bolt upright!

MONSTER FUN

How do you know that smoking is harmful to your health?
Well, look what happened to all the dragons!

Should monsters eat people on an empty stomach?
No, they should eat them on a plate!

What is monsters' favourite party game?
Swallow the leader!

Why don't skeletons sing church music?
They have no organs.

What goes 'WOO-HA-HA' THUMP?
Frankenstein's monster laughing his head off.

MONSTER FUN

What job does Dracula have with the Transylvanian cricket team?
He looks after the bats!

Why do ghosts never feel guilty?
They have a clear conscience!

First friend: Did you know that you can get fur from a vampire?
Second friend: Really? What kind of fur?
First friend: As fur away as possible!

Why do vampires dislike computers?
They hate anything new-fang-led!

Why did the car stop when it saw the monster truck?
It had a nervous breakdown.

Why was young Dr Frankenstein so popular?
Because he was great at making new friends!

How did you know I was a ghost?
Oh, I can see right through you!

How did the ghostly teacher make sure his pupils had learned what he had written on the board?
He went through it again!

Why did the monster buy an axe?
Because he wanted to get a-head in life!

How do vampires get clean?
In a blood bath!

What do trainee witches do at school?
Spelling tests.

What is the name for a group of vampires?
A fang club!

Why are vampires good at treating people with coughs?
Because they can clear your throat in seconds!

How do big, hairy monsters eat their dinner?
They wolf it down!

Why did the two vampire bats get married?
Because they were heels over heads in love!

MONSTER FUN

Why do ghosts go back to the same place every year for their holiday?
They like their old haunts best!

Did you hear about the hip-hop mummy?
He was a wrap artist!

What do the police call it when they watch a vampire's house?
A stake out!

Where did Dracula open his bank account?
At a blood bank!

What will a vampire never order in a restaurant?
Steak.

MONSTER FUN

Why wasn't the werewolf astronaut allowed to land his spaceship?
Because the moon was full!

Who do vampires invite to their birthday parties?
Anybody they can dig up!

Why did Dracula advertise for a housekeeper?
He wanted some new blood in the house!

Who is the world's scariest superhero?
Vampire bat-man!

What sort of telescope lets you see ghosts?
A horrorscope!

What do you call a lazy skeleton?
Bone idle!

What did Frankenstein do when the monster's head kept falling off?
He made a bolt for it!

Why do monsters like to stand in a ring?
They love being part of a vicious circle!

Where do werewolves live?
In warehouses.

Why doesn't Dracula have any friends?
Because he's a pain in the neck!

What does Dracula drink?
De-coffin-ated coffee!

'Hurry up,' said the father skeleton to his son, 'or you'll be late for the skull bus!'

What do you call a kind, helpful monster who likes flowers and butterflies?
A failure!

What did the old vampire say when he broke his teeth?
Fangs for the memory...

What does it say on the mummy's garage entrance?
Toot, and come in!

MONSTER FUN

Who was the winner of the headless horse race?
No one. They all finished neck and neck!

Why are you throwing garlic out of the window?
To keep vampires away.
But there aren't any vampires here.
See – it works!

Why did the giant robot feel sick after eating a train?
He caught a commuter virus!

If having hairy palms is the first sign
of turning into a
monster, what is
the second?
Looking for them!

Why did Godzilla stop
eating buildings?
He got atomic ache!

MONSTER FUN

What do ghosts do if they are afraid?
Hide under a sheet!

Why did the monster have twins in his lunchbox?
In case he felt like seconds!

Why didn't the vampire laugh at the joke about the wooden stake?
He didn't get the point!

Why did the werewolf swallow a bag full of pennies?
Because he thought the change would do him good!

Why do zombies always look so tired?
They are dead on their feet!

What is the first
thing a monster
eats when he
goes to a
restaurant?
The waiter!

What do monsters call a
crowded swimming pool?
Soup!

Why did the robot need a
manicure?
He had rusty nails!

Why didn't the
phantom win the
lottery?
He didn't have a ghost of a chance!

Why do football teams have to practise so much when
they play against zombies?
Because they face stiff competition!

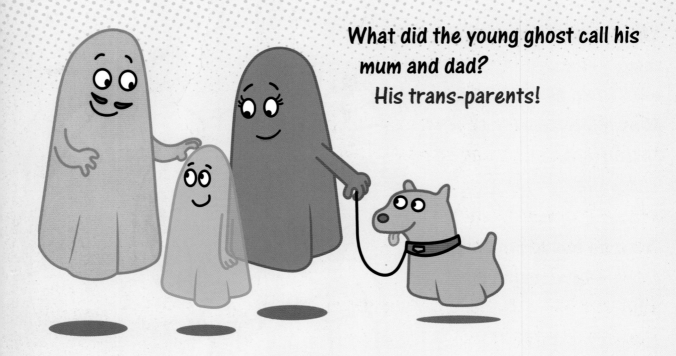

What did the young ghost call his mum and dad?
His trans-parents!

Why do little monsters not mind being eaten by ghosts?
Because they know they will always be in good spirits!

Why are there more ghost cats than ghost dogs?
Because every cat has nine lives!

Why do monster parents tell their children to eat their cabbage?
Because they want them to have a healthy green complexion!

MONSTER FUN

Which monster is the most untidy?
The Loch Mess Monster!

Why did the cyclops school close down?
Because they only had one pupil!

Why are vampires stupid?
Because blood is thicker than water!

Why do other monsters find mummies vain?
They're so wrapped up in themselves.

Why do vampires never invite trolls to their
dinner parties?
They can't stand all that goblin!

MONSTER FUN

What do you call a ghostly chicken?
A poultry-geist.

Why did the zombie go to the pharmacy?
He wanted something to help stop his coffin.

What do you call a kid vampire?
A pain in the knee!

Who do vampires invite to their weddings?
All their blood relatives!

MONSTER FUN

How does a skeleton know when it's going to rain?
He just gets a feeling in his bones!

Why don't ghosts do aerobics?
Because they don't want to be exorcised!

Why are owls so brave at night?
Because they don't give a hoot for ghosts, monsters or vampires!

How do vampires show affection for each other?
They bat their eyelids!

What is the first thing you should put into a haunted house?
Someone else!

Why did Goldilocks go to Egypt?
She wanted to see the mummy bear!

What did the werewolf say to the skeleton?
It's been so nice getting to gnaw you!

Why did the ghost go to the bicycle shop?
He needed some new spooks for his front wheel!

What do you get if you cross the Abominable Snowman and Count Dracula?
Severe frostbite!

What did the witch call her baby daughter?
Wanda!

What do you need to pick up a giant's cutlery?
A forklift.

MONSTER FUN

What do you call a male vampire in women's clothing?
Drag-cula!

How do you make a skeleton laugh?
Just tickle his funny bone.

Knock knock!
Who's there?
Russia!
Russia who?
Russia way – a monster's coming!

Why was the genie in the lamp angry?
Someone rubbed him up the wrong way!

MONSTER FUN

What do you get if you cross a warlock and a laptop?
A computer wizard!

What do skeletons say before eating?
Bone appetit!

What do you call the jewels that ghosts wear?
Tombstones!

What do dinosaurs rest their teacups on?
Tyrannosaucers.

MONSTER FUN

How do you help Frankenstein's monster?
Give him a hand when he needs it!

How do witch children listen to stories?
Spellbound!

How can you tell
when a robot
is angry?
It flips its lid!

What flavour drink do
monsters slurp?
Lemon and slime.

Book spotted at the
school library:
'The Haunted House', by Hugo First.

What do you call a hairy monster that's lost
its way home?
A where-am-I wolf.

What happens when a witch catches the flu?
Everyone gets a cold spell!

Why do vampires have a steady nerve?
They are as ghoul as cucumbers!

Why don't vampires write their own books?
They prefer to use ghost writers!

Where do monsters like to go on holiday?
Death Valley!

MONSTER FUN

Why do sea monsters go to so many parties?
Because they always have a whale of a time!

What do you call monster children?
Ghouls and boils.

How did the mother monster stop her son from biting
his nails?
She cut his fingers off.

Mummy, mummy, what is a werewolf?
Be quiet and comb your face!

What do abominable snowmen sing at parties?
'Freeze a jolly good fellow...'

MONSTER FUN

Why are monsters forgetful?
Because everything goes in one ear and out the others.

What do baby sea monsters play with?
Doll-fins!

What happened when the yeti ate a curry?
He blew his cool.

What is a vampire's favourite animal?
A giraffe.

What do mummies do to relax?
They just unwind a little!

Why can you
never get
through to a
vampire bat
on the phone?
Because they always
hang up!

Why did King Kong
climb the Empire State Building
in New York?
He wanted to catch a plane.

What kind of mistakes do young ghosts make
at school?
Boo-boos.

What was the name of the ghost who ate too much
porridge?
Ghoul-dilocks.

Why are so few ghosts ever arrested?
Because it's so hard to pin anything on them.

MONSTER FUN

What do you call a
little monster with a
wooden leg?
A hoblin-goblin.

Why are vampires
such good
comedians?
Because of their
biting wit.

What happened to
the naughtiest witch
in the class?
She was ex-spelled!

Which monster has the best hearing?
That depends on which one is the eeriest.

Why don't witches wear sombreros?
Because there's no point.

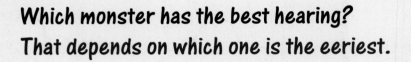

MONSTER FUN

What pets does Dracula own?
A bloodhound and a ghoul-fish!

What happened to the ghostly comedian?
He was booed off the stage.

What happened to the ghost
who got lost in the fog?
He is now sadly mist.

Why do skeletons hate
winter?
Because the cold goes right
through them!

Why did King Kong join the
army?
To learn about gorilla
warfare.

Glossary

aerobics exercises that keep your body in shape

atomic to do with atoms, the basic unit that everything is made from – or the energy that comes from atoms

banshee a wailing spirit from Irish folk tales

complexion the way the skin of your face looks

exorcise to drive a ghost or spirit away from a place

goulash a meat and vegetable soup from Hungary

Further Reading

Horsfall, Jacqueline. *Giggle Fit: Dinosaur Jokes*. Sterling Publishing, 2004.

Howell, L. *Monster Jokes*. Usborne Publishing, 2004.

Winter, Judy A. *Jokes About Monsters*. Raintree, 2010.

Index

Websites

CBBC 'Crack a Joke' game: www.bbc.co.uk/cbbc/shows/cbbc-jokes

Jokes by Kids website: www.jokesbykids.com

Yahoo! Kids Jokes: http://kids.yahoo.com/jokes